IN THE BEGINNING . . .

# The Liverpool Scene

edited by Edward Lucie-Smith

1968

Doubleday & Company, Inc.

Garden City, New York

**To the Beatles**
**without whom &c**

*821.9*
*L937l*
*1968*

Photographs on pages 2, 14, 20–21, 28,
42, 78–79, 80, 98, 113, 114–115 and
118–119 by Philip Jones Griffiths; photograph on page 89 by Frazer; photograph
on page 91 by Marilyn Stafford; photograph on page 49 by Graham Keen.


*The Liverpool Scene* was originally published by Rapp & Carroll, Ltd., London,
in 1967. The Doubleday paperbound edition is the first United States publication.
Doubleday edition: 1968

This book is in some ways an experiment. The chief innovation is that I have interspersed the poems not only with photographs of the poets and their surroundings, but with direct quotations taken from tape-recordings made with the three poets who are most heavily represented in it. I have also included a small number of quotations from other sources. What I have tried to do is to establish a kind of texture, both social and verbal, in which the poems take, quite naturally, the predominant place. The attitudes expressed by the three poets towards 'oral poetry' tended to be a little contradictory (and self-contradictory) as the attentive reader will see. However, it does seem to me that, essentially, the poetry now being written in Liverpool differs from other contemporary English verse because it has made its impact by being spoken and listened to, rather than by being read. The text of a given poem will often turn out to be fluid—the poet adapts it to suit the circumstances of a particular performance. It was this air of fluidity and spontaneity which I wanted to preserve. The recordings were not formal interviews so much as rambling conversations with the machine as an eavesdropper—the excerpts I print here are the reactions of the moment, not considered formal statements. In short, I have attempted to convey as much as possible of the 'scene' which surrounds and informs both the poets and their poems.

E.l.-S.

## Introduction

I was talking to someone from Liverpool about this book. 'You must remember,' he said, 'that in the provinces there are no schools of thought. You don't have people sitting at other people's feet, saying "I think you're right." In London, you can learn all about culture in a dull sort of way. In the provinces, you're given culture in school, which you either accept or reject. You can't go and visit somebody and say: "I've come to see you about culture." If you experience anything at all, for the first time, it's an original thought to you. There's nobody to follow, in the provinces.'

Parts of this speech may be obscurely phrased, but I think it contains a good deal of truth. The poems in this book are interesting from many points of view, but the most important thing is that they should speak for themselves, and, speaking thus, should bring into question a good many of our current assumptions about the arts and the place which they have in our society.

Ever since the war, there has been a good deal of talk about broadening the cultural base, bringing art to the people, taking art to the provinces. One thinks not only of such enterprises as Joan Littlewood's abortive fun-palace and Arnold Wesker's Centre 42, but of the Government's still fairly recent White Paper on the future of the arts. An essential phrase in all discussions of the subject was the one about 'getting people to participate.' No one seems to have thought that any kind of spontaneous generation could take place; nor that such art, if it arose, might bring into question accepted standards.

The 'Liverpool scene' of this book seems to have been born in the very early sixties. Pete Brown, more usually associated with jazz-and-poetry readings in London and the south of England, gives a lively account of it:

'Well, this is the poetry thing really: I mean the atmosphere and the people were there already, definitely, and it was very sort of ripe. Late in 1960 Spike Hawkins and I were living in London but we met up with a team of people from Liverpool at the Beaulieu Jazz Festival in 1960 and they said, you know, that things were good up there and that we should come up and sort of enjoy ourselves. Well, Spike and I got into conditions of extreme and dire poverty, so one night he hitched up there and accepted the invitation. They had this coffee bar there which was run by a very extraordinary guy—it was named after some Victorian, Liverpool Victorian person, Mr. Somebody Streate, and was called Streate's Coffee Bar because of this painting they had of him there. This guy that used to run it was a very good guy. That was the centre of activity and meetings. Finally, Spike and another guy called Johnny Byrne, who's an Irishman who was living in Liverpool at the time and was a friend of Adrian Henri's—they started these readings up there. The readings—well, Adrian, in fact, hadn't written any poetry for about six or maybe more years before that—he knew all about it, of course, you know, the things that were happening in poetry—but he just hadn't written any, and Brian Patten and Roger McGough were completely and absolutely unknown, and the fact of having regular sessions at this place brought them into the light and made Adrian start writing again. This was early '61. That's how the poetry thing in Liverpool began, certainly, because I mean Roger and Brian just turned up at respective times when we were there and asked if they could read—things like that. And Roger at the time was a schoolteacher and Brian was, as far as I know, oh well, he was a cub reporter on the *Bootle Times*.'

Needless to say, various points in this account are contested by other people who claim to have been on the spot. But it does provide a kind of picture of the place, the atmosphere, the time—and of circumstances very different, say, from those which surrounded the poets of 'the Movement,' then at the very height of its popularity.

Any discussion of Liverpool poetry has to turn soon enough to the city itself, if only because of the curious love-hate relationship which seems to exist between the poets and the place. Liverpool is very much present in most of the poems printed in this book—not only its various monuments, the street names and so forth, but in the very turns of speech and the attitudes to life which they express. To the outsider, the city has a strangely derelict air. There are many stretches of featureless rubble, many broken windows, many buildings in bad repair. As recently as 1875, the Canning Street quarter was described as 'the best-built and most respectable quarter of what may be called intra-mural Liverpool'—a description which scarcely anyone would credit now. Liverpool, and especially the district I have just mentioned, is a city of many graffiti; some obscene, other curtly witty. It is also—and this is important—very predominantly working-class. People with money move out to the Green Belt on the other side of the Mersey. There is none of that wealth which you still occasionally get a sniff of in Manchester or Leeds.

But the city continues to think of itself as something pretty special. 'The most obvious thing about Liverpool at the moment,' says the informant I first quoted, 'is that they have a lot of feathers in their cap—not only from the poetry point of view, or the pop point of view, but even from the football point of view.' Liverpool knows its own standards, and imposes them firmly. Its inhabitants are gifted with a famous sarcasm.

All of this might be thought of as inimical to the poet, instead of which we find the phenomenon of a group of poets—small enough, it's true, and till recently without connections in the world of London publishing (most of them, in fact, have seen very few of their poems in print)—who have still managed to establish themselves, and who have found an enthusiastic local audience.

In order to account for this one has to turn to the world of pop. Such torrents of drivel have been written about pop music, pop culture and pop art since the advent of the Beatles that one is reluctant to rake the whole subject up again. Yet there are one or two things which seem to me worth noticing. For example, the fact that the success of the Beatles had a seismic effect on provincial culture as a whole. For the first time London had been left out in the cold till the very last minute. The upsurge of the groups went on for a long time after the Beatles had established themselves as international idols. The journalists and the investigators came, and entertainers in Liverpool were suddenly provided with an acceptable identity.

Some of this glory was reflected on to the poets. If poetry was a branch of show business, it became, in Liverpudlian terms, respectable. I put some stress on this because of the attitude which Liverpool writers often express towards the label 'poet.' Roger McGough talks of the fact that a poet tends to keep quiet about his work in Liverpool, and is reluctant to put himself forward too obviously. Yet poetry in Liverpool is more uninhibitedly colourful, more deliberately 'public,' than at any other place in the British Isles. McGough himself belongs to The Scaffold, a satirical group with a rising reputation. He is very insistent about the importance of professionalism. Mike Evans is a member of a well-known beat group, The Squares; Brian Patten earns most of his living by doing readings.

The poets obviously value the enthusiasm of their young Liverpool audiences because this is a reassurance in more than one sense. It helps to prove that they have not cut themselves off from their environment, have not sold out to middle-class culture. The kind of poetry printed in this book is the sort which is often ignorantly labelled 'beat.' It's quite true that poets in Liverpool, like poets in other provincial cities in Britain (London is far more resistant), have felt a strong current of influence from America, and particularly from Ginsberg. What one doesn't find is that complete disgust with society and the established order of things which can be heard ever more shrilly in the American mimeographed magazines: 'Poet X,' says a reviewer in a recent issue of one of these, 'is unspoiled, not suckered-in, sold-out, diverted, smothered, or saved.'

Yet, having established this rapport with their local audience, the Liverpool poets seem to tread some curious paths. How is it, for example, that an affectionate, half-frivolous, half-serious cult of Batman and Superman can be combined with an equally affectionate cult of Jarry's Père Ubu? And where does this strange mish-mash of references come from—to favourite pop songs, to Félix Fénéon, Peter Pan and Napoleon Solo? The answer seems to lie in several places. For instance, there is the lack of cultural hierarchies which I've already referred to. Tennyson and Jarry are both equally astonishing, if you happen to come to both of them more or less unprepared and at the same instant. Several poets spoke to me of their resistance to the kind of poetry which had been offered to them in school, and the sudden revelation when they encountered such writers as Rimbaud and Baudelaire. The point about such writers was that they were moving, not that they practised a particular style, or advocated a particular way of writing. And the impulse was to pair these discoveries off, not with other writers (in the accepted literary way), but with other things which were thought of as moving, such as the pop songs of the moment. The criterion was not so much what a thing was, but what it did; and this, as we shall see later, is an important distinction.

Of course, when one begins to look at things closely there are some odd correspondences. The traditional brutality of Liverpool humour is especially close to Jarry. McGough's 'Monika' lyrics seem to have a natural, rather than a forced, affinity to Apollinaire. But it is the least 'respectable' sources which provide some of the most interesting insights. The poems in this book which I imagine are most likely to irritate certain readers are the ones which celebrate the folk heroes of pop —Batman, Superman, and the rest. How outrageous, for example, is the cool admission by one of the poets that these are simply fashionable images borrowed from metropolitan newspapers! One kind of cynicism, or so it would seem, has simply been added to another. Is this the case? Batman and the rest must certainly, by force of circumstances, have enjoyed a genuine place in the childhoods of most of the poets represented here. The comic-strip heroes were always ersatz; the loyalty given to them was, once upon a time, genuine. As Brian Patten says, in one of the poems printed here:

We killed them all simply because we
   grew up;
Who made them possible with our
   uneducated minds
And with **our** pocket money
And with the sixpences we received
For pretending to be Good.

When the revival came, a good many of the Liverpool poets seem to have experienced a moment of ironical delight. The mythology of the deprived, ramshackle and decrepit as it now was, had suddenly been given a place of honour in the drawing-rooms of the middle-class. The poems which the Liverpool poets write about Batman and Superman seem to me to be a celebration of unease, of ambiguous feelings—not so much towards the old world of the comic strips as towards the new celebrators and promoters of comic-strip values down there in the south of England.

The relationship between metropolitan and provincial culture is, in fact, one of the basic themes of this book. Poets in Liverpool, like provincial writers and artists everywhere in England, seem to hover between two contradictory sets of attitudes. London inspires fear and resentment—a fear of being brushed aside, a resentment of slights either real or imagined. It also arouses mockery for its inhibitions and its pretentiousness. Liverpool poets feel a real sympathy for their environment, but an even greater loyalty. They are still astonished by the miracle (as it seems to them) of a growing local audience. A man trying to write poetry in Liverpool usually has the attitudes of a frontiersman: life is harder, but in some ways cleaner and better. It is more genuine, closer to essential values. One must add to this the Liverpudlian sense of innate superiority which I have already mentioned.

People often talk about the metropolitan view of events in the provinces; they seldom, it seems to me, attempt to describe the provincial view of what happens in London. I am not, I know, especially well qualified to do this, but I am prepared to try. First of all, there is, I believe, a certain puzzlement over the distinctions which are made in the metropolis between high art and low. Beat music, for instance, is not regarded in Liverpool (at least among the young public who listen to it) as merely entertainment, as a background noise. The connoisseurship of beat groups and their various styles can be almost as refined as the connoisseurship of opera at Covent Garden. It is, however, demonstrably less articulate. But then, so is the reaction to poetry. Poetry and the music of the beat groups are accepted on the same level of experience; no distinction is made between the two forms. Indeed, the audience is hardly conscious that there *is* a distinction: the poetry and the music are judged by precisely the same criteria. It is important, then, to stress that these criteria spring perfectly naturally from the environment. What is missing in Liverpool, as indeed elsewhere in the provinces, is the condescending falsity with which all pop manifestations tend to be discussed in metropolitan newspapers. For better or worse, the audience is not aware that there is anything which needs to be condescended to.

The tendency to assume that entertainment and art are more or less the same thing has had disastrous consequences in the past. There is, nevertheless, something which needs to be said about the situation as we now find it. To return for a moment to the tricky theme of pop culture: it seems to me that what people really mean when they use this phrase is the process of democratization, accelerated by the swift diffusion of words and images which modern communications have made possible. They also mean (and here the term becomes pejorative) that culture has in some way sold out and become entirely subject to commercial laws of supply and demand, to the pressures of fashion and obsolescence. Yet one does find, among the poets represented in this book, both a fascination with pop materials and a determination to apply standards to them and to what is done with them. Adrian Henri says: 'On the one hand you can't not take the audience into account, and on the other you don't write purely and simply to impress the audience.' Brian Patten goes further: 'I believe in poetic entertainment, but poetic entertainment is not poetry, it's not sort of big enough, you know.'

The difficulty lies not in the absence of standards, but in the fact that the standards being applied are in some ways different to those which prevail in the metropolis. During the past ten years or so there has been a great deal of literary activity in English provincial cities. There has been a great proliferation of duplicated magazines and so forth. But all this has turned not towards London, but towards America, for a good part of its ideas. There has never been a time, I think, when young poets in the provinces have been so bored and impatient with the work held up to them as an example by the reviewers in London. A. Alvarez's famous attack on 'the gentility principle,' which prefaces his anthology *The New Poetry*, is regarded as a kind of ironic joke.

From the provincial point of view, and most especially from the Liverpool point of view, metropolitan judgments are a mixture of the academic and the moralistic, and both of these qualities are thought to be profoundly unsympathetic if not laughable. The 'how to' aspect of a great deal of recent reviewing—the meticulous verbal analysis which derives from the American 'New Critics,' from Yvor Winters, and from Leavis and Empson—this is regarded as wrong-headed. Truth to feeling is valued much higher than truth to language. At the same time, a bad poem is not necessarily regarded as a crime. The shrill indignation of the Sunday and weekly reviewers, when a poet fails to measure up to their particular prescription for good poetry, is thought of as an expenditure of emotional energy which is entirely beside the point.

This may seem to represent a retreat towards the criteria of incoherence—'it swings, man, it swings.' Certainly the strength of academic methods of judgment is that they provide a fixed point of reference. The painstaking analysis of detail forces the critic to establish a logical framework—not only must he judge, but he must try to relate one judgment to another. But there is a corresponding weakness, which would be seen more clearly if literature did not tend to be thought of (at any rate in England) as something entirely *sui generis*, and unconnected with the other arts. And perhaps, after all, English literature has remained surprisingly isolated from the main current. The immense developments which have taken place in painting and music have tended to pass the writer by.

Granted the crudity of most art criticism, which usually does not compare in subtlety with what the literary critics have to say, one can still point out that the art critic has a wider frame of reference, and that he has to face certain implications which the critic of literature can still contrive to ignore. I spoke just now of the tendency of the poets who are represented in this book to judge a poem not so much by what it was as by what it did. The effect which the poem produces is more important than the poem itself. If one can usefully make such a distinction, the poem is no longer an artifact, or a commodity, but a service; it is an agent rather than an object. In French literature this tendency stretches a long way back—as far as Rimbaud and Baudelaire. It is significant that these are precisely the writers whom some of the Liverpool poets choose to mention when groping for a definition of what they want to do.

If one wants to account for the fact that such a development should take place in the provinces rather than in London, one has to go back, I think, to that absence of hierarchies which I began with. For example, Adrian Henri, in many ways the central figure in the 'Liverpool scene,' is a painter and teacher of art. It is interesting that there is no such thing as an 'art world' or a 'poetry world' in this context. Banded together against the provincial environment, artists and writers exist as a single group, sharing one another's company, and also one another's ideas. If one wants to find a modern equivalent of Murger's *Vie de Bohème*, one has to look for it in Liverpool.

This comparison may seem an odd enough way of recommending a group of poets for their modernity. Murger's view of art and literature is, at first sight, a long way distant from anything which we would think of as contemporary. The paradox is that, on the Continent, and even to some extent in America, artists and writers have continued to keep one another company. One has only to look at the history of Cubism, of Dada, of Surrealism, to see how important the association of the various arts has been. It is only in Eng-

land that a kind of segregation has been enforced. This segregation was bound to lead to a kind of enfeeblement. To do them justice, the critics of poetry have not been slow to spot this, though they have not known precisely where to lay the blame. If English attitudes towards poetry have been largely negative during the fifties and sixties, it is because poetry itself has adopted negative or defensive postures. We have, in fact, been living in a period of literary counter-revolution, with all the lack of flexibility which this implies.

What I am trying to say is that I admire the poems in this book because, basically, they make no pretensions to being invulnerable, and because they seem to me to be written by people who are more interested in life than in literature. Sentimentality, coarseness of texture, carelessness with details—all of these are things which are present in full measure. What the reader has to decide for himself is whether these form an insuperable barrier to enjoyment. Even at their most casual and surrealist, these poets always give the impression of being real people at grips with real and pressing situations. Theirs is not the only sort of poetry one can write, but at least it seems to me a poetry which is worth reading, and which seems to foreshadow developments which are bound to take place in both our literature and our society as a whole.

Edward Lucie-Smith

EDWARD LUCIE-SMITH (IN LIVERPOOL)

# The Poems

# The Photographs

## from Leland's 'Itinerary,' 1533-9

Lyrpole, alias Lyverpoole, a pavid Towne, hath but a chapel. The King hath a Castelet there, and the Erle of Darbe a Stone Howse there. Irisch Marchauntes cum much thither as to a good Haven.

## from Camden's 'Britannia,' 1586

From Warrington the Mersey grows broader, and soon after contracts itself again; but at last opens into a wide mouth very commodious for trade, and then runs into the sea, near Litherpoole, in Saxon Liferpole, commonly called Lirpoole, called so (as 'tis thought) from the water spread like a fen there. It is the most convenient and frequented place for setting sail into Ireland, but not so eminent for its being ancient, as for being neat and populous.

## from an anonymous late 18th century account

Those who from necessity are affianced to a spot, are amused and gratified by their improvements and public erections, which, from a located prejudice and partiality, they too often believe equal to those in other parts of the kingdom; but while such improvements may satisfy their ambition and contribute to their convenience, they may give neither invitation nor amusement to any but those who are immediately interested in their concerns. Impartiality and historic justice declare Liverpool to be completely within this description; their buildings and places of amusement may please the natives, but they have neither novelty nor a superior elegancy to attract the notice of the judicious itinerant, and are consequently deficient in essentials to embellish the historic page.

## from the same account

. . . the liberal arts are a species of merchandise in which few of the inhabitants are desirous to deal except for exportation.

## Brian Patten talking

Liverpool is a sort of—it's a city. I mean I feel I belong here. I've got a sort of—what's its name?—got a sort of complex about it—Oedipus complex, I expect.

## Liverpool *after William McGonigal*


O Liverpool on the Mersey River
Noble city, how I shiver
With pride at the thought of your history
And your great men who are gone
Like Huskisson, and Mr Gladstone.
After each you have named a dock
From Bootle to the Liver clock
And some miles further on,
Even to Dingle and gay Garston.

You are the second greatest port in all
                                    the land,
And your population runs to eight hundred
                                    thousand.

Twenty miles of busy docking
Thanks to all the good men working
On them. The brave stevedores
And men in crane-driving
Have helped to make this great port thriving.

Your flour mills and other famous industries,
Biscuit, pea, soap and sugar factories,
All play a very important part;
And of all industrial south-west Lancashire,
Liverpool is the very heart.
Noble city astride the River Mersey,
I am sure we all salute thee.


*Roger McGough*


**Roger McGough talking**
Liverpool's like the cowboy frontier.

# Liverpool 8

Liverpool 8 . . . A district of beautiful, fading, decaying Georgian terrace houses . . . Doric columns supporting peeling entablatures, dirty windows out of Vitruvius concealing families of happy Jamaicans, sullen out-of-work Irishmen, poets, queers, thieves, painters, university students, lovers . . .

The streets named after Victorian elder statesmen like Huskisson, the first martyr to the age of communications whose choragic monument stands in the tumbledown graveyard under the cathedral . . . The cathedral which dominates our lives, pink at dawn and grey at sunset . . . The cathedral towering over the houses my friends live in . . .

Beautiful reddish purplish brick walls, pavements with cracked flags where children play hopscotch, the numbers ascending in silent sequence in the mist next morning . . . Streets where you play out after tea . . . Back doors and walls with names, hearts, kisses scrawled or painted . . .

Peasants merrymaking after the storm in Canning Street, street musicians playing Mahler's Eighth in derelict houses . . . White horses crashing through supermarket windows full of detergent packets . . . Little girls playing kiss-chase with Mick Jagger in the afternoon streets . . .

A new cathedral at the end of Hope Street, ex-government surplus from Cape Kennedy ready to blast off taking a million Catholics to a heaven free from Orangemen . . . Wind blowing inland from the
Pierhead
bringing the smell of breweries and engine oil from ferry boats . . .

*Adrian Henri*

**Adrian Henri talking**
There's no money in Liverpool, there's no loot at all.

**Swaqk** *Liverpool soundpoem*

Forswaqk sqaukn torqt?
Adswaqktion rapt swaqts the bare
sswaqkts-round-the-face/cataswaqkt pulted gheists
und geheinzsqakst vorpt im yovvel!
Swakquorn huntuch untouched towels, vowels yevorrn
imswaqk heswakg I saw swaqk, I saw swaqksaw
whackigon the railroad down swaqked a truck
and off came his rose,
down swaqked a truckdoor and cracked off his nose

*Pete Brown*

## Roger McGough talking

In Liverpool you're a poet one minute, but the next minute you're talking about football, or you're buying bus tickets, or someone's kicking your head in outside of a pub. It's all part of living. If you have an experience you go home and write the poem about that experience, then you go out and get drunk, or you meet friends and things.

## Rain

All through the summer
  I wanted to be an engine driver
But after the rain
  I wanted to be a Beatle.

*Mike Evans*

# Limestreetscene '64

Turned left into Lime Street
felt small
like a pelota ball

St George's Hall
black pantheonic
like a coalman's wedding cake
glows in the neonic
presence of Schweppervescence
and 'Guinness is good for you'

Proud buses turn up Skelhorn Street
and vomit and dribble up the hill
once more to fill
their 'no smoking' 'spitting forbidden' bellies.
Ahoy Doris, docker's delight
with cheeky breasts and indelible lips
tempting by
smart as paint
from your evilheels
to your brothelblackhair
laying a perfumed trail of gin
Irish linen and men

**Allen Ginsberg talking**
. . . Liverpool, which I think is at the
present moment the centre of the con-
sciousness of the human universe.
They're resurrecting the human form
divine there—all those beautiful youths
with long, golden archangelic hair.

Outside the Chinese cafes
like buddhas bouncers stand
lest a band
of teds or sailors
or drunken Viking whalers
should seek to violate the chow mein
and trample on the waterchestnuts
Turned left into Brownlow Hill
felt big
as a pig

*Roger McGough*

**Mrs Albion You've Got a Lovely Daughter** *for Allen Ginsberg*


Albion's most lovely daughter sat on the banks of the Mersey
    dangling her landing stage in the water


The daughters of Albion
    arriving by underground at Central Station
    eating hot ecclescakes at the Pierhead
    writing 'Billy Blake is fab' on a wall in Mathew Street

    taking off their navyblue schooldrawers and
    putting on nylon panties ready for the night


The daughters of Albion
    see the moonlight beating down on them in Bebington
    throw away their chewing gum ready for the goodnight kiss


sleep in the dinnertime sunlight with old men
    looking up their skirts in St John's Gardens

    comb their darkblonde hair in suburban bedrooms
    powder their delicate little nipples
    wondering if tonight will be the night

    their bodies pressed into dresses or sweaters
    lavender at The Cavern or pink at The Sink


The daughters of Albion
    wondering how to explain why they didn't go home


The daughters of Albion
    taking the dawn ferry to tomorrow
    worrying about what happened
    worrying about what hasn't happened
    lacing up blue sneakers over brown ankles
    fastening up brown stockings to blue suspenderbelts

*Beautiful boys with bright red guitars*
*in the spaces between the stars*

Reelin' an' a-rockin'
Wishin' an' a-hopin'
Kissin' an' a-prayin'
Lovin' an' a-layin'

Mrs Albion you've got a lovely daughter

*Adrian Henri*

ADRIAN HENRI

# I say I say I say

I say  I say  I say
a funny thing happened on my way here today
the buildings had hiccoughs the roads ran away
Buses grew hairs in the most private places
traffic lights chuckled and pulled funny faces
Hot-bladdered lampposts chased little dogs
the moon took a hiding from stars wearing clogs
Policemen threw helmets at innocent stones
as cheeky boys laughed and broke words with bones
The lions in Lime Street have started to roar
A poet's not safe out alone anymore

*Roger McGough*

## Adrian Henri on Allen Ginsberg

Ginsberg has so much bloody personality that you can't ignore him: the man stands up and talks to you and you sit there and listen. He had a fantastic effect on Liverpool. He was very different in London—he was very tied-up there. The great thing here was that nobody knew who he was—you take him to the pub and all you get is these guys saying, 'Who's that funny fellow with you, the fellow with the long hair?' And Allen would just stand there and talk to you for five minutes and just wander away and you'd see him talking to somebody and then he'd wander off and talk to somebody else. And hundreds of people kept coming here for weeks afterwards, saying 'Hey, that American bloke with the long hair who was with you—he's gear, isn't he?' You know, all sorts and conditions of funny people whom you wouldn't expect to were terribly impressed by him. And the musicians, you know—we took him to The Cavern, and he went up to The Cavern office afterwards and got into a discussion with two drummers from beat groups, and brought out his finger-cymbals and was playing all these Tibetan rhythms and they thought this was great.

**The New 'Our Times'** *for Félix Fénéon*

1
At 3 p.m. yesterday a Mr Adolphus Edwards, a Jamaican immigrant, was pecked to death by a large bronze eagle in Upper Parliament Street. A U. S. State Dept. spokesman said later: 'We have no statement to make as of this time.'

2
Police-constable George Williams, who was partially blinded by a 15-lb. jellybaby thrown at a passing pop singer, is to be retired on half pension.

3
Bearded Liverpool couple put out of misery in night by drip oil-heater, court told.

4
A certain Mrs Elspeth Clout, of Huyton, was killed by an unidentified falling object. It was thought to be a particularly hard stool evacuated from the toilet of a passing aeroplane.

5
Two chip-shop proprietors were today accused of selling human ears fried in batter. One of them said: 'We believe there is room for innovation in the trade.'

6
Fatality in Kardomah bomb outrage: Waitress buried Alive under two thousand Danish pastries.

7
At the inquest on Paul McCartney, aged 21, described as a popular singer and guitarist, P. C. Smith, said, in evidence, that he saw one of the accused, Miss Jones, standing waving bloodstained hands, shouting, 'I got a bit of his liver.'

*Adrian Henri*

# The day before yesterday

The day before yesterday as I was walking down Dale Street
a small man, a complete stranger, seeking to prove his
existence through an intense traumatic experience
leapt off a bus & fired a bullet point-blank into my
forehead.

      (it was terribly embarrassing)

I stifled a scream & pulled my hat down over
my eyes but could not prevent the blood from ruining
my new Raelbrook shirt & vertical-striped Italian jacket
with brass buttons.

But the traffic stopped & little boys took their hands
out of their pockets & little girls wet themselves,
& young brides had orgasms & old people were disgusted
at the extrovert behaviour of this gentleman
swaying & bleeding in good old Dale Street.

      (it was terribly embarrassing)

Not wanting to annoy people any further I
lurched through the crowd & stumbled into the Kardomah Cafe
just down the road. The girl behind the counter was very
nice when I ordered coffee & a hamroll but explained that
I was making a mess of the Danish pastries & could I take
my dripping carcass elsewhere.

      (it was terribly embarrassing)

I bubbled my apologies & followed a young gentleman
about to be sick into the gentlemen's where unobtrusively
& with as little fuss as possible I gave up the ghost.

*Roger McGough*

## Roger McGough talking

If you're, say, between the age of 15 and 98, and you say: 'I'm writing poetry', you wouldn't think of going to London, you'd stay in Liverpool, because Liverpool is a scene now. Ten years ago one would have gone towards where the poetry scene was— to London.

## from Williamson's 'Liverpool Advertiser', 1765

To be sold at auction at George's Coffee-House, betwixt the hours of six and eight o'clock, a very fine negro girl about eight years of age, very healthy, and hath been some time from the coast. Any person willing to purchase the same may apply to Capt. Robert Syers, at Mr Bartley Hodgett's, Mercer and Draper near the Exchange, where she may be seen till the time of sale.

## Problems

1
Question:
Someone
with a parcel
is running for a bus
(the parcel is very heavy).
Should he drop it?
And so make certain
of getting home all right
for sure? Or
should he struggle
with the parcel
and maybe miss the bus?
(He may
get the parcel into the bus,
which he had taken for granted
that he would,
before he suddenly saw
that he may not.)
Which then
is worse?
To arrive home
without the parcel
or to be stuck
with it
at the bus stop
and no bus?

Answer:
It depends what's in the parcel.
2
It is a scene of stillness.
There is a man standing
at a bus stop.
He is looking into the distance.
He knows what time it is.
Resting under his hand is
a large parcel.

There is nothing to suggest
that there will be a bus stopping
there soon, that the man is aware
of the bus stop, or that
the parcel belongs
to the man.
What will happen?

*Heather Holden*

**Roger McGough talking**
I don't think it's a Liverpool thing as
opposed to a Newcastle thing or a
Birmingham thing; I think of it as a
Liverpool thing as opposed to a London
thing, or a capital thing, or a public
school thing. You're far more involved
in the setting, you're far more involved
in the city in Liverpool than you would
be in London, for instance. Every day
you walk out of your flat and you walk
round Liverpool, and you know everywhere you're going, you know every
skyline and every gutter, every person
and every street, every crook and nan-
nie.

# M 61

        The politicians
(who are buying huge cars with hobnailed
wheels the size of merry-go-rounds)
        have a new plan.
        They are going to
        put cobbles
        in our eyesockets
        and pebbles
        in our navels
        and fill us up
        with asphalt
        and lay us
        side by side
so that we can take a more active part
                        in the road
        to destruction.

*Roger McGough*

**Tonight at Noon** *for Charles Mingus and the Clayton Squares*


Tonight at noon
Supermarkets will advertise 3d EXTRA on everything
Tonight at noon
Children from happy families will be sent to live in a home
Elephants will tell each other human jokes
America will declare peace on Russia
World War I generals will sell poppies in the streets on November
11th
The first daffodils of autumn will appear
When the leaves fall upwards to the trees

Tonight at noon
Pigeons will hunt cats through city backyards
Hitler will tell us to fight on the beaches and on the landingfields
A tunnel full of water will be built under Liverpool
Pigs will be sighted flying in formation over Woolton
and Nelson will not only get his eye back but his arm as well
White Americans will demonstrate for equal rights
in front of the Black House
and the Monster has just created Dr Frankenstein

Girls in bikinis are moonbathing
Folksongs are being sung by real folk
Art galleries are closed to people over 21
Poets get their poems in the Top 20
Politicians are elected to insane asylums
There's jobs for everyone and nobody wants them
In back alleys everywhere teenage lovers are kissing
in broad daylight
In forgotten graveyards everywhere the dead will quietly
bury the living
and
You will tell me you love me
Tonight at noon


*Adrian Henri*

# The death of Nelson tipped

Don't worry about me
save the women and children,
the cafe is going down with all hands
while my feet are awash in cold tea.

Nearer my god to thee
and with one foot in the gravy,
I batten down the mashed potato hatches
against the appalling waves of rice pudding.

Horatio is there, lying near the cash
desk with what appears to be custard
dribbling down his chin; kiss him for Christ's
sake, and let's heave him overboard.

Now thousands of Zulus are streaming
out of the kitchens and pelting us with
bread rolls, this thin red line of bent
old men can't last much longer.

To hell with Nelson, and the women and
children, I'm getting out of here before
this ketchup on my shirt turns into blood.

*Henry Graham*

## Adrian Henri talking
The Beatles were the first cultural
phenomenon of any kind who made it
outside London first.

# For you everything's gonna be all right

For you everything's gonna be all right

For you they'll redecorate the city . . .
put a lampshade around the sun
and whitewash the clouds
Hoover the streets
and wallpaper the buildings

For you they'll convert
crematoriums into supermarkets
and graveyards into playing fields
ambulances into ice-cream vans
and hospitals into fun palaces

For you policemen will take off
their bruise-coloured uniforms and command respect
by the width of their navels
Policewomen will go to bed
handcuffed to their teddy bears

Old age pensioners will be allowed into
lunchtime sessions at The Cavern for half-price

The queen will head the bill
at the London Palladium
Val Parnell will foot the bill
at the London Palladium

Maurice Woodruff will make a fortune

Armand and Michaela Denis will stop beating
about the bush

Billy Graham will be the next pope

Liz Taylor in her next big motion picture
will pick her nose

Mr Vorster will refuse to appear
on coloured television

They will give Vietnam back to the Irish

The Red Army will devote itself entirely
to show business

For you everything's gonna be all right

For you politicians will identify themselves
by pulling tongues at blind ex-servicemen
Detective inspectors will identify themselves
by wearing S.S. uniforms
Prostitutes will identify themselves
by loitering on all fours
Queers will identify themselves
by walking backwards

For you all first-born American boys
will be christened Hiroshima

For you the next Miss Universe
will have been a thalidomide baby

For you they will make adultery
an offence punishable by knighthood

For you they will discover
that there is no such thing as history

For you they will discover
that the cure for cancer is masturbation

For you marijuana will be on sale in the foyer

For you everything's gonna be all right

For you, sorrow
will be the broken necklace you only keep
for sentimental reasons
the absurd hat you bought but never wore

For you, death
will be the dirty underskirt one only sees
hanging from other girls
the randy salesman who only calls when
you're not at home

I will hold you gently like broken fruitcake
I will let you come but never go
I will love you forever . . . forever . . . for you . . .
everything's gonna be for you . . . all right

*Roger McGough*

## Roger McGough talking

We've got no literary or dramatic heritage. We try out what we're doing, and we test it on people, and people react, and we sort of go on from there. We haven't got people to bow down to. The Beatles were like that—they liked certain things, they liked Little Richard, but they didn't know anything about music.

*ROGER MCGOUGH AND ADRIAN HENRI*

## Don't worry/Everything's going to be all right

Don't worry
If your boyfriend doesn't treat you right
baby
Everything's going to be all right
come with me
And every poem I write will have your name in it
Don't worry
If the factories and villas cover the countryside
Everything's going to be all right
England will be given back to the animals
and we'll find a home under fern leaves known only to
    foxes
Don't worry
If I can't afford to buy you coffee after school
Everything's going to be all right
Soon the poem will replace the pound sterling
As international currency
and Britain will get on the poem standard again
Don't worry
About those lunatics in the government
Everything's going to be all right
The country will be governed by beautiful girls under 18
(and you will let me carry your portfolio home from the
    House)
Don't worry
About what happened the other night
Everything's going to be all right
They'll give you contraceptive pills shaped like
    jellybabies with your milk at playtime
Don't worry
About what your Dad says about the younger generation
Everything's going to be all right
There'll be involuntary euthanasia for everyone over 30
    not a poet painter or musician

Don't worry
About the rain
Everything's going to be all right
The streets will be covered with tiny pink flowers
like the ones on your suspenderbelt
Bathing suits will be banned from beaches
School uniforms will be the only kind allowed in public
Your end-of-term report will be marked out of 100 for
    sex appeal
(and you will be Top of the Form)
Policemen will be beaten up by poets
Trade Unions will be taken over by workers
There'll be 24-hour licensing
And everyone will be on the National Drink Service
Your parents will wake us every morning with breakfast
Your teacher will smile at notes saying we stayed in bed
    late
Your face will be in every art gallery
Your name in every book of poetry
So
Don't worry
Everything's going to be all right.


*Adrian Henri*

ADRIAN HENRI

### In the Midnight Hour

When we meet                    I remember
in the midnight hour
country girl                     Your cold hand
I will bring you nightflowers    held for a moment among strangers
coloured like your eyes         held for a moment among dripping trees
in the moonlight                in the midnight hour
in the midnight
hour                            I remember

Your eyes coloured like the autumn landscape
walking down muddy lanes
watching sheep eating yellow roses
walking in city squares in winter rain
kissing in darkened hallways
walking in empty suburban streets
saying goodnight in deserted alleyways

in the midnight hour

Andy Williams singing *We'll Keep a Welcome in the Hillsides*
for us
when I meet you at the station
The Beatles singing *We Can Work It Out*
with James Ensor at the harmonium
Rita Hayworth in a nightclub singing *Amade Mia*

I will send you armadas
of love vast argosies of flowers
in the midnight hour
country girl

when we meet

in the
moonlight
midnight
hour
country girl

I will bring you

yellow
white
eyes
bright
moon
light
mid
night
flowers

in the midnight hour.                                    *Adrian Henri*

## Where are you now, Superman?

The serials are all wound up now,
Put away in small black boxes
For a decade or so. Superman's asleep
In the sixpenny childhood seats,
Batman and Robin are elsewhere
And can't see the Batsign thrown out
By kids with toffee-smeared mouths.
Captain Marvel's SHAZAM! echoes round the auditorium,
But the magicians don't hear him,
Must all be dead . . .

The Purple Monster who came down from the Purple Planet,
Disguised as a man, is wandering aimlessly about the streets
With no way of getting back.
Sir Galahad's been strangled by the Incredible Living Trees,
Zorro killed by his own sword.
Blackhawk's buried his companions
In the disused hangers of innocence
And Flash Gordon likewise wanders lonely,
Weeping over the girl he loved 7 universes ago.

We killed them all simply because we grew up;
Who made them possible with our uneducated minds
And with our pocket money
And the sixpences we received
For pretending to be Good.
We think we are too old to cheer and boo now,
But let's not kid ourselves,
We still cheer and boo
But do it quietly or at General Elections
Where it's still possible to find a goodie
Now and then.

Clark Kent (alias Superman)
Committed suicide because he failed to find new parts.
The bullets that bounced off him on the screen
Wormed their way in to Real Life.
But who cared then for real life?

We had our own world with our own celluloid imaginations
And now we have a different world,
One that's a little more cynical
And that we are convinced is more real.

Our batsignals now questions flung into space
To attract the attention of passing solutions . . .


*Brian Patten*


**Roger McGough talking**

The Batman, Superman, comic-strip thing always comes second-hand, I think, to Liverpool. First of all you read about it in *The Observer*, and the scene-chiefs take it up in Liverpool very quickly, and they tell all about it far quicker than they probably do in London. In London, unless you've seen the Batman films you can't really talk about it; in Liverpool, someone tells you second-hand. Second-hand knowledge in Liverpool is first-hand experience.

## Goodbat Nightman

God bless all the policemen
and fighters of crime,
May thieves go to jail
for a very long time.

They've had a hard day
helping clean up the town,
Now they hang from the mantelpiece
both upside down.

A glass of warm blood
and then straight up the stairs,
Batman and Robin
are saying their prayers.

They've locked all the doors
and they've put out the bat,
Put on their batjamas
(they like doing that)

They've filled their batwater bottles
made their batbeds,
with two springy battresses
for sleepy batheads.

They're closing red eyes
and they're counting black sheep,
Batman and Robin
are falling asleep.

*Roger McGough*

**Batpoem** *for Bob Kane and The Almost Blues*


Take me back to Gotham city
                Batman
Take me where the girls are pretty
                    Batman

All those damsels in distress
Half-undressed or even less
The BatPill makes 'em all say Yes
                    Batman

Help us out in Vietnam
             Batman
Help us drop that BatNapalm
               Batman

Help us bomb those jungle towns
Spreading pain and death around
Coke n' candy wins them round
               Batman

Help us smash the Vietcong
              Batman
Help us show them that they're wrong
                  Batman

Help us spread democracy
Get them high on LSD
Make them just like you and me
               Batman

Show me what I have to do
             Batman
'cause I want to be like you
             Batman

Flash your Batsign over Lime Street
Batmobiles down every crimestreet
Happy Batday that's when I'll meet
             Batman

*Adrian Henri*

## Adrian Henri's Talking After Christmas Blues

Well I woke up this mornin' it was Christmas Day
And the birds were singing the night away
I saw my stocking lying on the chair
Looked right to the bottom but you weren't there
  there was
    apples
      oranges
        chocolates
          . . . aftershave
—but no you.

So I went downstairs and the dinner was fine
There was pudding and turkey and lots of wine
And I pulled those crackers with a laughing face
Till I saw there was no one in your place
  there was
    mincepies
      brandy
        nuts and raisins
          . . . mashed potato
—but no you.

Now it's New Year and it's Auld Lang Syne
And it's 12 o'clock and I'm feeling fine
Should Auld Acquaintance be Forgot?
I don't know, girl, but it hurts a lot
  there was
    whisky
      vodka
        dry Martini (stirred
          but not shaken)
            . . . and 12 New Year resolutions
—all of them about you.

So it's all the best for the year ahead
As I stagger upstairs and into bed
Then I looked at the pillow by my side
I tell you baby I almost cried
   there'll be
      autumn
         summer
            spring
               . . . and winter
—all of them without you.


*Adrian Henri*

ADRIAN HENRI

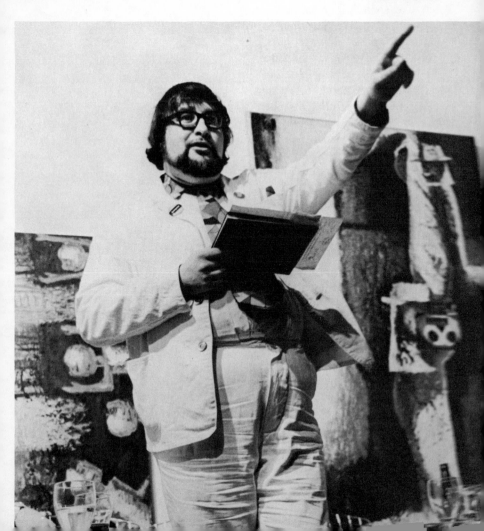

## Mother, there's a strange man waiting at the door

Mother,
There's a strange man waiting at the door
with the familiar sort of face you feel you've seen before.
Says his name is Jesus
and can we give 'im 'alf a crown
says 'es run out of miracles
and now 'is luck is down.
Yes I think 'e is a foreigner
Egyptian or a Jew.
Oh aye and that reminds me
'ed like some water too.
Well, shall I give 'im what 'e wants
or send 'im on 'is way?
All right I'll give 'im sixpence.
Say that's all we've got today
and I'll forget about the water.
I suppose it's a little bit mean
but 'onest 'es filthy dirty
you don't know where 'es been.

Mother, he asked about the water
I said we 'adn't got a cup.
Anyway I give 'im the tanner
'e really was made up.
Said it was little things like that
that kept 'im on the rails.
Then 'e gave me 'is autographed picture
and these three rusty nails.

*Roger McGough*

**Roger McGough talking**
One must get away from poetry as
something that happens where there's
a glass and a bottle of water.

50

## I've had a lousy Xmas

I have had a lousy Xmas
I have had enough of chicken's legs
  and breasts and parsons' noses
  of mistletoe and white draining-board sandwiches.
I have raped a packet of 'pleasurable Players'
  (to symphonic accompaniment)
  and have drunk
  five million bottles of Guinness
  (daily).

I have had a lousy Xmas
I have driven a tinfoil turkey
  through the jolly, hollied streets of Liverpool
  shouting: 'Get stuffed'
  to the plum-duffed little people
  the mince-pied
  pie-eyed little people
  dying in their decorated parlours.

I have had a lousy Xmas
I have received presents
  from all my enemies:
  a portrait of the Queen
  back copies of *Encounter* and *London Magazine*
  a bar of Lifebuoy toilet soap
  a gamekeeper's outfit
  and an LP of this poem.

At tea on Boxing Day
I pulled a cracker
  and out popped dead North Vietnamese
  and South Vietnamese
  and I wept
  into my trifle.
I have had a lousy Xmas
  because I believe in Santa Claus
  and someone's gone
  and crucified him.                    *Roger McGough*

**Before it happened**


A week before it happened the president of the united
states woke from his bed smelling of warm american
soil and opened the curtains and saw that there were
no longer any flowers on the lawns of the white house.

A week before it happened russia declared Mayakovsky
a saint and showered his grave with forget-me-nots
. . . a religious parchment was unearthed in a small
village outside jerusalem. Its message was simple and
direct and nobody could translate it . . . remains of atlantis
were discovered inside a dead volcano . . .

A week before it happened an Unidentified Flying Object
bombed america with itching powder; groups of children
out on picnics accidentally discovered and exploded bombs
and themselves; crowds committed mass love in city streets.

Six days before it happened the president found that the
grass on the lawns of the white house had rotted away.
The forget-me-nots forgot both russia and Mayakovsky
before the two faded leaving only their smell as evidence.

Five days, and now migrating birds block out the sunlight
over london, all canvasses at the tate are empty . . . All
paintings at the official war museum explode.
Park lakes like tainted microfilms; no swans, wind, fish
or children swimming.

Four days before it happened pale and lyrical couples
wandered into stables, bedrooms, empty cinemas and other
places of refuge for a final Good Time. The last frankenstein
film has been shown to an audience of mutants, the final
scene mutilated by the tears of the projectionist.

On the last days all bedroom doors turned back into trees
smothering the sleeping population with damp leaves. Only
those who could hibernate survived. The rest decayed.

*Brian Patten*

BRIAN PATTEN

**Brian Patten talking**

You want to communicate it. I don't know why you want to communicate, don't really know that. I expect there's a very simple reason. . . .

**Brian Patten talking**

I've been trying to get something about the city into my poems. I'm amazed I'm on this, this city with winds and grass blowing through, and it's like being on a planet, and this planet is in this universe, and the clouds are going past me, you know. It's a fantastic feeling. I'm trying to get this in my poems. Mainly lyric, the hard lyric.

## Roger McGough talking

I think poetry is about whatever one feels like in this particular poem. I think generally when people write about the Bomb and things it's too big, you know, too vast, to think about. I'm concerned about the person next door and the person next to me. I'm involved in a very claustrophobic environment—or envirusment!—rather than wide social things. . . . The Georgian poets were poets who tended their gardens while the factories were being built on the outskirts; in fact, what we're doing is that—while the mushroom cloud is growing outside on the horizon we're laying the birds in the back yard.

## Mother, the wardrobe is full of infantrymen

Mother, the wardrobe is full of infantrymen
i did, i asked them
but they snarled saying it was a man's life

Mother, there is a centurion tank in the parlour
i did, i asked the officer
but he laughed saying queen's regulations,
piano was out of tune anyway

Mother, polish your identity bracelet
there is a mushroom cloud in the back garden
i did, i tried to bring in the cat
but it simply came to pieces in my hand
i did, i tried to whitewash the windows
but there weren't any
i did, i tried to hide under the stairs
but i couldn't get in for civil defence leaders
i did, i tried ringing Candid Camera
but they crossed their hearts

I went for a policeman but they were looting the town
i went out for a fire engine but they were all upside down
i went for a priest but they were all on their knees
mother don't just lie there say something please
mother don't just lie there say something please

*Roger McGough*

## Good luck to you Kafka/You'll need it boss

the man from the finance company
came again today he wants to know
when i'm going to pay but what he won't say
is what it was i bought

one morning perhaps when i was high
on poetry and corned jock butties
i must have wandered threepartsmental
into a departmental store and bought something

a three-piece suite for my sweet
a frigidaire to keep frozen my despair
a fitted carpet for the inside of my head

he just won't say what it was
and when i laugh he looks the other way
apparently i have only fourteen days left
he won't even say what happens then

i suppose they will come and take away my eyes
(which i know i haven't paid for)
or the words that live inside my head
or my surprise at raindrops or the use

of my legs or my love of bread
then again they just might forget
about me and go away/fat chance


*Henry Graham*

## The world's first junior executive

The world's first junior executive,
Now 87 years old, sits alone in his study
Looking outside, where, it seems, buildings
Are collapsing on one another, and he
Still alone these years on
Draws up the final schedule,
The final business transaction
Between man and God.

This morning the dawn hesitates over Woolworth's
Wondering whether to disturb his phallic dreams
Or let them go on.
Birds of love that once flew in pairs
Now make singular journeys—
He who was not brave about living
Is less brave about dying;
Still, he dies.
And in various offices new executives rise
Not in 'silent tribute'
But to cough and apply
For what his death
Has left open to them.

*Brian Patten*

## Sad Aunt Madge

As the cold winter evenings drew near
Aunt Madge used to put extra blankets
over the furniture, to keep it warm and cosy.
Mussolini was her lover, her life
was an out-of-focus rosy-tinted spectacle.

>But neurological experts
>with kind blue eyes
>and gentle voices
>small white hands
>and large Rolls Royces
>said that electric shock treatment
>should do the trick
>it did . . .

Today after 15 years of therapeutic tears
and an awful lot of ratepayers' shillings
>down the hospital meter
>sad aunt madge
no longer tucks up the furniture
>before kissing it goodnight
>and admits
that her affair with Mussolini
>clearly was not right
particularly in the light
of her recently announced engagement
>to the late pope

*Roger McGough*

## Little Johnny's confession

This morning
      being rather young and foolish
      I borrowed a machine gun my father
      had left hidden since the war, went out,
      and eliminated a number of small enemies.
      Since then I have not returned home.

This morning
      swarms of police with tracker dogs
      wander about the city
      with my description printed
      on their minds, asking:
      'Have you seen him,
      he is seven years old,
      likes Pluto, Mighty Mouse
      and Biffo the Bear,
      have you seen him anywhere?'

This morning
      sitting alone in a strange playground
      muttering you've blundered, you've blundered
      over and over to myself
      I work out the next move
      but cannot move.
      The tracker dogs will sniff me out,
      they have my lollipops.

*Brian Patten*

### Brian Patten talking

I don't really think of the audience, no. It just happens. But some of the things I write about, some of the images I use, are recognizable. When it works it's real for me, you know, it's real. I don't think about whether it's going to be real for anybody else. I mean if it's real, it's real! If I've created something, that's real. It doesn't change: it stays real. If other people see it as real, that's up to them.

## Little Johnny takes a trip to another planet

Through his bedroom window, later they confirmed,
Johnny drifted one Monday evening
Up above the sleeping world.

He left this message:

I've taken a trip to another planet
So I'll be away for awhile,
Don't send the Escaped Children Squad after me,
The universe is too wild.

Now among black glass trees
He weaves intricate shapes
In a world an inch away from ours,
And from behind his eyes
He sees into a waiting room of light
And maps out the route dawn takes through
The nurseries of night.

He has switched on a world and walked inside,
And as silence blooms among the flowers
He wonders are people groping through
Transparent hours;
For though Peter Pan has petered out
And Wendy's lost her glow
He still considers carefully
What Captain Hook could never know . . .

So don't send the Escaped Children Squad after him,
He'll be away for awhile,
He's taken a trip to another planet
And the universe is too wild
For him to make it back
In the same state of mind.


*Brian Patten*

## Little Johnny's foolish invention

One day
      while playing with old junk in the attic
      Little Johnny accidentally invented an atomic bomb
      and not knowing what to do with it
      buried it in the front garden

Next morning
      during cornflakes and sunrise
      he noticed it glowing damp among the cabbages
      and so he took it out
      out into the city
      where it smelt of tulips
      but was sadly inedible

What can I do with it, he sighed, having nowhere to hide it?
I'm afraid that soon a busy policeman will come along
To detain me. I'd make a statement. Say
I'd like a new bomb a blue bomb an anti-war bomb
A bomb I could explode in dormitories where my friends
      are sleeping

That would not wake them or shake them
      but would keep them from weeping,
A bomb I could bounce in the playground
      and spray over flowers,
That would light the universe for years and send down
      showers of joy.

      But he'd pay no attention
      Would take out his notebook and write
      This child is mad
      This child is a bomb . . .

Last night in my nightmares the bomb became transparent
and through it my atomic friends walked naked
except for a few carefully placed leaves
that were continually rotting

So now looking much older I trace about obscure cities
looking for a place to leave my bomb, but am always
          turned away
by minor politicians who say it's a deterrent. I answer,
          sure!

It will deter flowers and birds and the sunlight
          from calling
and one morning during sunrise when I rise and glow
I will look outside to make sure my invention has
          not bloomed
but will see nothing through the melted windows . . .


*Brian Patten*


## Little Johnny's final communication


Mother,
          I won't be home this evening, so
          don't worry; don't hurry to report me missing.
          Don't drain the canals to find me.
          I've decided to stay alive, don't
          search the woods I'm not hiding,
          I've simply gone to get myself classified.

          Don't leave my shreddies out,
          I've done with security.
          Don't circulate my photograph to society,
          I have disguised myself as a man
          and am giving priority to obscurity.

          It suits me fine, I have taken off my short trousers
          and put on my long ones
          and now am going out into the city, so
          don't worry; don't hurry to report me missing . . .


*Brian Patten*

## Roger McGough talking

I write poetry in various ways—either the word, or the image, or the idea, I suppose. A line starts me off—say a line like: 'Monika, the tea things are taking over.' I think of the line then I try to work out what follows from the line. I never think of the poems in terms of performance, actually, but I sometimes think, writing a poem, that this will be dramatic, you know, or best performed dramatically, and then one tends to write more loosely than one does for the page.

## Monika, the tea things are taking over

Monika, the tea things are taking over!
the cups are as big as bubblecars
they throttle round the room
tin openers skate on the greasy plates
by the light of the silvery moon
the biscuits are having a knees-up
they're necking in our breadbin
that's jazz you hear in the salt cellars
but they don't let non-members in
the eggspoons had our eggs for breakfast
the sauce bottle's asleep in our bed
I overheard the knives and forks
'it won't be long,' they said
'it won't be long,' they said

*Roger McGough*

# Take it off

Something's got to be done
and done right away
Monika don't argue
do as I say

I've put out the milkman
and wound up the maid
it's well after midnight
so don't be afraid

The bed's in a mess
perhaps you'd better shake it
no, not that dear,
not when you're naked

yes leave the light on
there's so much to see
now Monika take your wig off
and lie next to me

*Roger McGough*

SPIKE HAWKINS

## Ten milk bottles standing in the hall

ten milk bottles standing in the hall
ten milk bottles up against the wall
next door neighbour thinks we're dead
hasn't heard a sound he said
doesn't know we've been in bed
the ten whole days since we were wed

no one knows and no one sees
we lovers doing as we please
but people stop and point at these
ten milk bottles a-turning into cheese

ten milk bottles standing day and night
ten different thicknesses and
different shades of white
persistent carolsingers without a note to utter
silent carolsingers a-turning into butter

now the wife's run out of passion
and there's not much left in me
so maybe we'll get up
and make a cup of tea
then people can stop wondering
what they're waiting for
those ten milk bottles a-queueing at our door
those ten milk bottles a-queueing at our door

*Roger McGough*

# It all started yesterday evening

It all started yesterday evening
as i was helping the potatoes
off with their jackets
i heard you making a date
with the kettle
i distinctly
heard you making a date
with the kettle
my kettle

then at midnight
in the halfnight
while i was polishing the bluespeckles
in a famous soap powder
i saw you fondling
the frying pan
i distinctly
saw you fondling the frying pan
my frying pan

finally at middawn
in the halflight
while waiting in the cool shadows
beneath the sink
i saw you making love
with the gas cooker
i distinctly
saw you making love
with the gas cooker
my gas cooker

my mistake was to leap upon
you crying:
'MONIKA SPARE THE SAUCERS'
for now you've left me
for someone
with a bigger kitchen

*Roger McGough*

# Three Poems Concerning Larionov's Provincial Life Series

## Target

My shoe has caught a pig!
My shoe has caught a pig!
I am a pig trap.

## Liddled

Pig fell over the upturned
motor car
Pig fell over the upturned
motor car
Drunk! said Pig
Drunk!

## Boiler

Pig sit still in the strainer!
Pig sit still in the strainer!
I must have my pig tea.

*Spike Hawkins*

# Me

*If you weren't you, who would you like to be?*

Paul McCartney Gustave Mahler
Alfred Jarry John Coltrane
Charlie Mingus Claude Debussy
Wordsworth Monet Bach and Blake

Charlie Parker Pierre Bonnard
Leonardo Bessie Smith
Fidel Castro Jackson Pollock
Gaudi Milton Munch and Berg

Belá Bartók Henri Rousseau
Rauschenberg and Jasper Johns
Lukas Cranach Shostakovitch
Kropotkin Ringo George and John

William Burroughs Francis Bacon
Dylan Thomas Luther King
H. P. Lovecraft T. S. Eliot
D. H. Lawrence Roland Kirk

Salvatore Giuliano
Andy Warhol Paul Cézanne
Kafka Camus Ensor Rothko
Jacques Prévert and Manfred Mann

Marx Dostoievsky
Bakunin Ray Bradbury
Miles Davis Trotsky
Stravinsky and Poe

Danilo Dolci Napoleon Solo
St John of the Cross and
The Marquis de Sade

Charles Rennie Mackintosh
Rimbaud Claes Oldenburg
Adrian Mitchell and Marcel Duchamp

James Joyce and Hemingway
Hitchcock and Buñuel
Donald McKinlay Thelonius Monk

Alfred, Lord Tennyson
Matthias Grünwald
Philip Jones Griffiths and Roger McGough

Guillaume Apollinaire
Cannonball Adderley
René Magritte
Hieronymus Bosch

Stephane Mallarmé and Alfred de Vigny
Ernst Mayakovsky and Nicolas de Stäel
Hindemith Mick Jagger Dürer and Schwitters
Garcia Lorca
            and
                    last of all
                    me.


*Adrian Henri*

MIKE EVANS

**Roger McGough talking**
I've had more plays on than I've been
to the theatre.

## Flood

*Woman:* If you weren't you who would you rather be?
  *Man:* If I wasn't me I would rather be the worst flood for years.
   *W.* A flood?
   *M.* A swollen river, a raging torrent.
   *W.* I'd never thought of you that way.
   *M.* An F-L-O-O-D smashing my way through railway lines,
       roads, homes, shops and across vast areas of farmland after
       48 hours of torrential rain.
   *W.* You'd make a handsome torrent.
   *M.* I'd burst my banks at 1 a.m. and race through the main
       street of your town.
   *W.* You often burst your banks about that time.
   *M.* I'd swirl around your house to a depth of several feet.
   *W.* You always were a deep one.
   *M.* Rising steadily. . . .
   *W.* I'd be upstairs in bed.
   *M.* Rising still further. . . .
   *W.* I'd get out and put on my Wellingtons.
   *M.* . . . . until I reached your bedroom window. . . .
   *W.* I'd open the window.
   *M.* . . . . and pour into your little room. (*Pause*)
   *W.* You'd have to kiss me first. (*Kiss*) Now ask me who
       I'd rather be if I wasn't me.
   *M.* Who would you rather be if you weren't you?
   *W.* If I wasn't me I would rather be Vera Lynn.
   *M.* Why?
   *W.* I don't know, I've always wanted to be Vera Lynn.


*Roger McGough*

71

# Adrian Henri's Last Will and Testament

*No one owns life, but anyone who can pick up a frying pan owns
    death.*

*William Burroughs*

To Whom It May Concern:

As my imminent death is hourly expected these days/
carbrakes screaming on East Lancs tarmac/trapped
in the blazing cinema/mutely screaming I TOLD
YOU SO from melting eyeballs as the whitehot fireball
dissolves the cathedral/behind the first human being to die of a
    hangover/
dying of over-emotion after seeing 20 schoolgirls waiting
at a zebracrossing:

I appoint Messrs Bakunin and Kropotkin my executors
and make the following provisions:

## I

I leave my priceless collections of Victorian oil lamps,
photographs of Hayley Mills, brass fenders and Charlie Mingus
records to all Liverpool poets under 23 who are also blues
singers and failed sociology students

## II

I leave the entire East Lancs Road with all its landscapes
to the British people

## III

I hereby appoint William Burroughs my literary
executor, instructing him to cut up my collected
works and distribute them through the public
lavatories of the world

## IV

Proceeds from the sale of relics—locks of hair, pieces
of floorboards I have stood on, fragments of bone
flesh teeth, bits of old underwear etc.—to be given
to my widow

## V

I leave my paintings to the nation with the stipulation
that they must be exhibited in public houses,
chip shops, coffee bars and cellar clubs throughout
the country

## VI

Proceeds from the sale of my other effects to be divided
equally amongst the 20 most beautiful schoolgirls in
England (these to be chosen after due deliberation and
exhaustive tests by an informal committee of my friends)

*Signed*
*Adrian Henri*
*Jan. 1964*

*witnessed this day by:*
  *James Ensor*
  *Charlie 'Bird' Parker*

## Adrian Henri:
## an oral autobiography

I was born in Birkenhead. I was an only child—a very weird life really—I was an only child till I was twelve and then my parents suddenly started having children. I'm one of a family of six—six kids—the youngest one is still at school. We lived in this terraced house in Birkenhead, horrible place, and we moved to North Wales just before the war. My father was a very badly paid minor civil servant—he's retired now—and I've always been incredibly poor. We lived in a council house thing. I went to grammar school, went to Dur-ham University, got a degree there: Fine Arts.

I worked in the fairground for ten summers altogether. My father was at the seaside, at Rhyl on the North Wales coast near Llandudno. When I was at school I started working there and when I was at college. But I did just everything: I worked on some of the rides, and one of those dive-bomber things, things where you strap people in at both ends and it whirls around. It's marvellous—if you feel bad you can scare the hell out of people. Marvellous

**73**

things we did: you get very sophisti-
cated, you sort of jam the brakes on
and fling it into reverse and it really
shakes people up; and also you develop
a technique whereby you whirl it
round very fast and when it gets going
you put the brakes on and let it more
or less get horizontal, you see, and all
the money in people's pockets slides
out and you whizz it round again and
all the money comes hurtling out. You
then set the machine to go on its own
and go out and collect the money . . .
I worked all the stalls. I had a catapult
stall for two years—I didn't own it, I
ran it for somebody; I just worked for
people. You had to burst balloons with
catapults, but the balls were made of
compressed cork so it was really very
difficult—you had to be immensely
strong.

What happened then was that I left
college and did teaching for six months
or something. I hated it: it was a Catho-
lic grammar school. I hated it. I decided
I didn't want to be a teacher, I just
wanted to be an artist, so I upped and
worked for two summers earning money
in the fairground and lived on it in
the winter. Then I came to live here in
Liverpool and worked in the theatre
for about six months as a scenic artist—
terrible, dreadful job. You do other
people's designs; it's just bloody hard
graft. You're a painter and decorator,
really, glorified. It did me good, I real-
ize now. You do things like you get a
30 ft. long and 20 ft. high thing which
you've just got to cover with white in

the morning. Eventually you cover this
area in about a quarter of an hour
when you get clever at it, and it stops
you being fiddly as a painter sort of
thing—a very loosening-up kind of
experience. The New Shakespeare was
open then and we did bits of work for
them. That was marvellous while it
lasted, that. The fate of that place is
fantastic. After the theatre company
packed in, it was used as a fruit ware-
house and there were protests about
this so then the city said it must be
used for cultural purposes. So it was
opened, so help me, as a night club!
But it suffered the fate of the Cities of
the Plain: it was only open one day
and it got burned down.

I worked in a public school, a minor
one, and then I worked in a grammar
school and then in a secondary modern
in Bootle—that was good but it was
terribly destroying. The kids were marvellous really, but you couldn't win.
You knew that everything was going to
get wrecked, everything you'd done. It
was a rehousing thing from Bootle and
they were very, very rough, these kids,
and the rest of the teachers in the
school were as thick as two short
planks anyway—they didn't have the
brains of a louse between them. Art
was *the* thing in the school: the kids
took to art like ducks to water. They
used to come back after school every
day and paint. There were twelve and
thirteen-year-olds doing oil paintings
and making all sorts of things. I even
ran a sort of Bauhausy basic course for

the final-year boys which they also used to do at home and that. That was marvellous.

Once you got out of the school there was nothing. They lived on this estate and there was literally nothing but houses and three shops and a big wilderness in the middle and nothing else—except two alehouses. So all the good that had been done just got undone when they got outside. Some kids were terribly good at it; they were never going to be artists or anything, but at least they were very sensitive and had very good ideas and things. And they became bread-van drivers and bread-van drivers' mates, if they were lucky, or the more literate ones got jobs as clerks in shipping offices and things like that. It was just terribly bringing-down to see what happened.

### Roger McGough talking

I was born in a working-class home where, if you're a poet, it's something to be ashamed of. Sort of thing one tells one's mother, and one's mother says you must get to be a teacher or something. You're a poet, and you write about things, and all the time you're not aware of being a poet in the sense that you can't go round saying that you're one, because people will say: 'That's nothing, lad. You should be a docker or a footballer or a film star or a guitar player.' In Liverpool, when you're a baby, they used to say: 'He's got good legs.' And now they probably say: 'He's got good arms, you know, long fingers.'

## Let me die a youngman's death

Let me die a youngman's death
not a clean and in-between-
the-sheets, holy-water death,
not a famous-last-words,
peaceful, out-of-breath death.

When I'm 73
and in constant good tumour
may I be mown down at dawn
by a bright red sports car
on my way home
from an all-night party

or when I'm 91
with silver hair
and sitting in a barber's chair
may rival gangsters
with ham-fisted tommyguns burst in
and give me a short back and insides

or when I'm 104
and banned from The Cavern
may my mistress
catching me in bed with her daughter
and fearing her son
cut me up into little pieces
and throw away every piece but one.

Let me die a youngman's death
not a free-from-sin, tiptoe-in
candle-wax-and-waning death
not a curtains-drawn, by-angels-borne,
'what a nice way to go' death.


*Roger McGough*

# A dream

Lying in bed this morning
I felt my power grow,
Adrenalin filled me from head to toe
Like a hot water bottle.
I was handsome, huge and virile.
The room was too small to contain me
            and too insignificant.

I sought to crash through the window
            into the backyard
            Leap over the wall
            into the entry
            Dash into the street
and out into the crashing blue sky of the world,

            to equate negroes
            and bait jewbaiters
            and eat atombombs
            and castrate dictators
            and resurrect God
            and prick egos
            and superprick superegos
            and uncripple cripples
            and marry lonely widowed women
            and widow lonely married women
            and give back the six counties. . . .
            and things like that
            while young girls marvel
            at the rippling potential of my body
            the tan glowing through my
                    chillprufe wyncyette
                        pyjamas.

Not wasting any more time
I hurled myself out of bed—BUT—
while fumbling for my glasses knocked them
on to the floor—AND—unable to find
them in the myopic midday gloom
            of my bedroom
            crawled back into bed
and dreamed instead powerful phallic dreams.

                                    *Roger McGough*

MURAL PAINTING (LIVERPOOL STYLE)

**Brian Patten talking**

I'm twenty. I started writing sort of verses in school but they never became poetry.

**Schoolboy**

Before playtime let us consider the possibilities
of getting stoned on milk.

In his dreams,
scribbling overcharged on woodbines,
mumbling obscure sentences into his desk:
'No way of getting out,
no way out . . .'

                Poet dying of
too much education, schoolgirls, examinations,
canes that walk the nurseries of his wetdreams;
satchels full of chewing gum; bad jokes, pencils,
crude drawings he passes for art. Soon will
come the joyful realizations in Mary's back kitchen.
All this during chemistry.

(The headmaster's crying in his study.
His old pinstriped pants rolled
up to his knees in a vain attempt to
recapture youth; emotions skid along
his slippery age; love, smeared across his face
like a road accident.)

The schoolyard's full of people to hate.
Full of tick and prefects and a fat schoolmaster
and whistles and older and younger boys, but
he's growing,
   sadly
      growing
         up.

CONTINUED OVERLEAF

Girls,
    becoming mysterious, are now more important
than arriving at school late or receiving trivial awards.
Postcards of those huge women
               seem a little more believable now.

(Secretly the pale—unmarried—headmaster telling him
Death is the only grammatically correct full-
                           stop.)

Girls,
    still mysterious;
arithmetic-thighed, breasts measured in thumbprints,
not inches.
Literature's just another way out.
History's full of absurd mistakes.
King Arthur never really existed
and if he had, he'd have only have farted and
excused himself from the Round Table in a hurry.
(The headmaster, staring through the study window
into the playground, composed strange poems about
the lyrical boy in class four.)

          'He invited us up sir,
        but not for the cane,
         he said the algebra of life
            was far too difficult to explain . . .'

Growing up's wonderful if
        you keep your eyes
         closed tightly

and if you grow
        take your soul with you,
             nobody wants it.

So,
playtime's finished with;
it's time to pull the last sad chain
                on his last
                        sadschoolgirlcrush.

It's time to fathom out too many things.
To learn he's no longer got somebody watching over him;
He's going to know strange things, learn
how to lie correctly, how to lay correctly,
how to cheat and steal in the nicest possible manner.
He will learn among other things how to enjoy
his enemies and how to avoid friendships. If he's unlucky
he will learn how to love and give everything away
and how eventually he'll end up with nothing.

        He won't understand many things.
He'll just accept them. He'll experiment with hard-boiled
                        eggs all his life
and die a stranger in a race attempting humanity.

    And finally,
the playground full of dust,
   crates of sour milk lining the corridors:
        the headmaster, weeping quietly among the saws
        and chisels
        in the damp woodwork room.

        The ghosts of Alan and Maureen and Peter
        and so many others,
   all holding sexless hands, and
one pale boy
in a steamy room
looking outside across the roofs and chimneys
where it seems the clouds are crying, and
the daylight's gone blind
and his teachers, all dead.


*Brian Patten*

## Brian Patten talking

It's just got to last longer than me. I'm involved with the poetry and music scene, and the entertainment. . . . I mean I believe in poetic entertainment, but poetic entertainment is not poetry, it's not sort of big enough, you know. Poetry is a private thing in itself. . . . I mean it's a gift as well so it should be given! It's not a lesson any more, really. It's nothing to do with that, it's nothing to do with educating or saying anything. As Auden says, the poet hasn't got a real place no more, he's just a person who's watching these things.

## What the littlegirl did

The littlegirl
 pulled up her bellyskin
  like a vest
   and examined her chest
    spleen, kidneys and the rest
     as a measled child a rash.

Sugar and spice
 and everything nice
  that's what littlegirls are made of.

So she put in a hand
 and pulled out a gland
  and said: 'What a strange girl am I'.


*Roger McGough*

## Love is . . .

Love is feeling cold in the back of vans
Love is a fan club with only two fans
Love is walking holding paintstained hands
Love is

Love is fish and chips on winter nights
Love is blankets full of strange delights
Love is when you don't put out the light
Love is

Love is the presents in Christmas shops
Love is when you're feeling Top of the Pops
Love is what happens when the music stops
Love is

Love is white panties lying all forlorn
Love is a pink nightdress still slightly warm
Love is when you have to leave at dawn
Love is

Love is you and love is me
Love is a prison and love is free
Love's what's there when you're away from me
Love is . . .

*Adrian Henri*

## Poem

The black-walled streets
will never be
the same
        again
the oily rains
that wash
the pavements
from Pierhead to Central
anoint me

A thousand visions
passed my eyes
before
I saw her
of clever eyes
        and talking

But through the
drunken haze
        she came
and it was
ONE WAY ONLY
from then
        on

Now I wear
a button-down
        heart
with her love
        on the
        inside
and a beat
        you can
        twist
                to.

*Mike Evans*

## Full of eastern promise

Oh yes,
we will eat spices
and sail down the
Brahmaputra
reading
the Kama Sutra.

*Heather Holden*

### Roger McGough talking

I failed English literature at Ordinary
level. When I went to the university I
did French and Geography. I did them
because I got the best marks in them,
you know—and Geography became
very scientific, and French became very
artistic. I suddenly realized that when I
was reading about people like Rimbaud
and Baudelaire, I felt as they felt. I
recognized a kindred spirit, and therefore I must be a poet, and therefore I
started writing poetry.

## At lunchtime, a story of love

When the bus stopped suddenly to avoid damaging
a mother and child in the road, the young lady in
the green hat sitting opposite was thrown across
me, and not being one to miss an opportunity I
started to make love with all my body.

At first she resisted saying that it was too early
in the morning and too soon after breakfast and that
anyway she found me repulsive. But when I explained
that this being a nuclear age the world was going
to end at lunchtime, she took off her green hat,
put her bus ticket in her pocket and joined in the exercise.

The buspeople, and there were many of them,
were shocked-and-surprised and amused-and-annoyed,
but when the word got around that the world was coming
to an end at lunchtime they put their pride in their
pockets with their bus tickets and made love one with
another. And even the bus conductor, being over,
climbed into the cab and struck up some sort of
relationship with the driver.

That night on the bus coming home
we were all a little embarrassed, especially me and
the young lady in the green hat, and we started to say
in different ways how hasty and foolish we had been.
But then, always having been a bit-of-a-lad, I stood up
and said it was a pity that the world didn't nearly end
every lunchtime and that we could always pretend.
And then it happened. . . .

Quick as a crash we all changed partners
and soon the bus was aquiver with white
mothball-bodies doing naughty things.

CONTINUED OVERLEAF

And the next day
and everyday
in everybus
in everystreet
in everytown
in everycountry
people pretended that the world was coming to an end
at lunchtime. It still hasn't. Although in a way it has.


*Roger McGough*


## Bang


And I never stopped
         running
from the day they told me
     the cowboys and indians
         at the
             bottom
                  of my garden
were all
         dead.


*Mike Evans*

## Poverty/sweet substitute

I've never slept with
anyone but you on
a floor she said but
after a while she
found someone with
a bed
instead

*Pete Brown*

## Buttons

Perhaps you don't love me at all,
but at least you sew buttons on my coat
which is more than my wife does.

*Adrian Henri*


## Parish boundaries

*Man:* I love you more than mountaintops love aeroplanes.
*Woman:* You're an old matchbox you are.
  *M.* If the world was roasted chicken I'd give you the breast.
  *W.* Ta very much, but don't think I'd give you any.
  *M.* I'd eat the parson's nose and give you all the rest.
  *W.* You're an old railway carriage, you are really.
  *M.* I want to know your secrets.
  *W.* They're secret.
  *M.* Secrets as secret as the shadows cast on your secret body.
  *W.* My legs are sealed.
  *M.* Forever?
  *W.* For you.
  *M.* Never.
  *W.* No, I was only kidding. You're cute really, even if you
      are an old dried milk tin.
  *M.* If you'd be Mrs Hopkinson my life would be one long
      round.
  *W.* You've been around.
  *M.* . . . of bread.
  *W.* Are you Mr Hopkinson?
  *M.* No.
  *W.* Oooh you're the city limits you are.
  *M.* Take off your parish boundaries.
  *W.* You're a primitive untamed dialogue.
  *M.* I know.
  *W.* And I love you for it.

*Roger McGough*

## Love poem/stomp

You stomped on me
& my entrails
spilled from my side
fortunately few
people saw as I
concealed them
in my handkerchief immediately

*Pete Brown*

## What you are

you are the cat's paw
among the silence of midnight goldfish

you are the waves
which cover my feet like cold eiderdowns

you are the teddybear (as good as new)
found beside a road accident

you are the lost day
in the life of a child murderer

you are the underwater tree
around which fish swirl like leaves

you are the green
whose depths I cannot fathom

you are the clean sword
that slaughtered the first innocent

CONTINUED OVERLEAF

*ROGER MCGOUGH*

## What you are

you are the blind mirror
before the curtains are drawn back

you are the drop of dew on a petal
before the clouds weep blood

you are the sweetfresh grass that goes sour
and rots beneath children's feet

you are the rubber glove
dreading the surgeon's brutal hand

you are the wind caught on barbed wire
and crying out against war

you are the moth
entangled in a crown of thorns

you are the apple for teacher
left in a damp cloakroom

you are the smallpox injection
glowing on the torchsinger's arm like a swastika

you are the litmus leaves
quivering on the suntan trees

you are the ivy
which muffles my walls

you are the first footprints in the sand
on bank holiday morning

you are the suitcase full of limbs
waiting in a left-luggage office
to be collected like an orphan

you are the musical queen
at attention
in a smoke-filled deserted cinema

you are a derelict canal
where the tincans whistle no tunes

you are the virgin's bottom drawer
full of pillowslips and crisp loins

you are the bleakness of winter before the cuckoo
catching its feathers on a thornbush
heralded spring

you are the stillness of Van Gogh
before he painted the yellow vortex of his last sun

you are the still grandeur of the Lusitania
before she tripped over the torpedo
and laid a world war of american dead
at the foot of the blarneystone

you are the distance
between Hiroshima and Calvary
measured in mother's kisses

you are the distance
between the accident and the telephone box
measured in heartbeats

you are the distance between power and politicians
measured in halfmasts

you are the distance
between the siren and the shrapnel
measured in splitseconds

you are the distance
between advertising and neuroses
measured in phallic symbols

you are the distance
between you and me
measured in tears

CONTINUED OVERLEAF

you are the moment
before the lovers met by chance
for the very first time

you are the moment
before the noose clenched its fist
and the innocent man cried: treason

you are the moment
before the warbooks in the public library
turned into frogs and croaked khaki obscenities

you are the moment
before the buildings turned into flesh
and the windows closed their eyes

you are the moment
before the railway stations burst into tears
and the bookstalls picked their noses

you are the moment
before the buspeople turned into teeth
and chewed the inspector
for no other reason than he was doing his duty

you are the moment
before the flowers turned into plastic and melted
in the heat of the burning cities

you are the moment
before the blindman puts on his dark glasses

you are the moment
before the subconscious begged to be left in peace

you are the moment
before the word was made flesh

you are the moment
before the clouds became locomotives
and hurtled headlong into the sun

you are the moment
before the television personality took off his trousers
and said: See I am just a man

you are the moment
before the spotlight moving across the darkened
stage like a crab finds the singer

you are the moment
before the seed nestles in the womb

you are the moment
before the clocks had nervous breakdowns
and refused to keep pace with man's madness

you are the moment
before cattle were herded together like men

you are the moment
before God forgot His lines

you are the moment
before we learned that the maninthemoon was
queer and some of us fled into the forests

you are the moment of pride
before the fiftieth bead

you are the moment
before the poem passed peacefully away at dawn
like a monarch


*Roger McGough*

HOPE STREET SIGN

**Brian Patten talking**

Whom do I read? No one specifically.
I mean certain poems, things like *Ode
to a Nightingale*. I like lyric poetry. I
like Ginsberg lyrics; I like Keats lyrics.
It's not the man, it's what he's saying
that interests me—and, of course, how
he says it. I like him to sing it!

## The fruitful lady of dawn

She walks across the room and opens the skylight
thinking perhaps a bird will drop in
and teach me how to sing.

She attempts to understand why a sentence made of kisses
is followed by the image
of somebody wandering alone through semi-colons

but cannot fathom out
whose dawn her heart belongs in;
so among them is silent

and under the skylight
puts on a red dress calling it a blue one;
she approaches breakfast as she would a lover,

she is alive,
and one of her body's commonest needs
I have made holy.

For she will feed my pink bird,
she will make love in Technicolor and will be
The Fruitful Lady of Dawn.

*Brian Patten*

## Said I trusted you

said I trusted you
spoke too soon
heard of your affair
with the maninthemoon
say it's all over
then if you're right
why does he call
at the house every night?

*Roger McGough*

## Party piece

He said:

'Let us stay here
Now this place has emptied
& make gentle pornography with one another,
While the party-goers go out
& the dawn creeps in
Like a stranger.

Let us not hesitate
Over what we know
Or over how cold this place has become,
But let's unclip our minds
& let tumble free
The mad, mangled crocodiles of love.'

So they did,
Right there among the Woodbines and Guinness stains,
& later he caught a bus, and she a train.
And all there was between them then
Was rain.                          *Brian Patten*

## Brian Patten talking
I've got no real urge to go to London. I mean I'd like to have enough money for me to be able to be totally independent of cities, independent of cities really, you know.

## Brian Patten talking
At the moment I'm doing a job. I don't really have to. It's just for extra money. Labouring in the park, looking after the flowers, cleaning lakes.

100

## Maud, 1967

Maud, where are you Maud?
With your long dresses and peachcream complexion;
In what cage did you hang that clack bat night?
What took place in the garden? Maud, it's over,
You can tell us now.

Still lyrical but much used, you wander about the suburbs
Watching the buses go past full of young happy people
Wondering where the garden is, wherever can it be,
And how can it be lost. Maud, it's no use.

Can it be that you got yourself lost
And are living with an out-of-work musician,
You share a furnished room and have an old wireless
That tells you the latest bad news.
What's happening, Maud?

Do you wear a Mary Quant dress?
Where are you? And are you very lost,
Very much alone? Do you have stupendous dreams
And wake with one hand on your breasts
And the other on your cunt?
Do you cry for that garden, lost among pornographic suggestions
Where the concrete flowers neither open nor close?
Who poured weed-killer over your innocence?

We could not find that garden for you,
Even if we tried.
So come into the city, Maud,
Where flowers are too quickly picked
And the days are murdered like vicious enemies.

Maud, is that you I see
Alone among the office blocks,
Head bowed, young tears singing pop-sorrow
On your cheeks?


*Brian Patten*

## Père Ubu in Liverpool

A Fragment

Time and Place:
Liverpool now

Dramatis Personae:
Père Ubu
Mère Ubu
Palotins
Liverpool bird
Mods
Man in bowler hat

*SCENE ONE*
(Père Ubu is discovered walking round the corner of Lewis's.)

*Ubu* (mopping brow):
By my green candle, we are excessively fatigued. (Sees bird
standing underneath statue.) Young lady, having recently
disembarked from that which crosses the water of the Mersey, we
are taking our Royal Person to your splendid Cathedral, which
will serve as our Phynancial Quarters, being of suitable
magnificence . . .

*Bird* (aside):
State of 'im!

*Ubu:*
. . . could you therefore direct the here-present Master of
Phynances to the building we have named?

*Bird:*
Yerwhar?

CONTINUED ON PAGE 105

*Ubu:*
Hornsgidouille, I cannot communicate with her. I shall try once
more . . .
Mademoiselle?

*Bird:*
Ooer!

*Ubu:*
Shittr! WHERE ARE WE?

*Bird* (comprehending):
Oh! Lewis's.

*Ubu:*
Ah. And that is no doubt a statue of Mr Lewis?

*Bird* (pointing upward and giggling):
What—*dar?* No. Dat's 'Scouse'.

*Ubu:*
And who is that?

*Bird:*
It's a statue of a feller with no clothes on and, er, all the fellers
meet their birds under it and when it's wet the rain drips off 'is
thingie and it looks as if he's . . . (dissolves into giggles)

*Ubu:*
I see. And where are you going, my dunderheaded maid?

*Bird:*
I'm meetin' me friend Mary and we're goin' to The Cavern.

CONTINUED OVERLEAF

*PÈRE UBU/ADRIAN HENRI*

*Ubu:*
Ah yes, I had heard there was a Cavern in the town.

*Bird:*
I'll 'ave ter go now—tarar!

(She hurries away, watched by Père Ubu. When almost offstage she drops her handbag, shouts 'ooer', picks it up again and exits.)

*SCENE TWO*
(The scene changes to Hardman Street. Père Ubu is discovered toiling up the hill, followed at a distance by Mère Ubu and a number of Palotins.)

*Mère Ubu:*
Oh, Père Ubu, you big bag of shit, why don't you ask someone the way?

*Ubu:*
Silence, Mère Ubu, or I'll wring your horrible scrawny neck. (Sees a crowd of Mods leaning against wall outside The Sink Club. Speaks to the nearest one.) Tell me, sire, could you direct me to that edifice known as the Cathedral?

*Mod:*
Yerwhar?

*Ubu:*
Hornsgidouille, shittr, can no one here speak a civilized tongue?

*Mod:*
Now then, la, yer wanner watch dat languidge yer know.

*Ubu* (to Mère Ubu and party):
Ignorant savages!

*Mod:*
Yer lookin' for a spot of lumber, la?

*Ubu:*
Lumber?

*Mod:*
You know—a bit of a barney, a punch-up, a KO job like.

*Ubu:*
Do you dare to challenge the mighty Master of Phynances himself to battle? The great Père Ubu, King of Poland, Count of Sandomir, Emperor of Liverpool! By my green candle, shittr, sire, a hideous fate shall be yours. Torsion of the nose and ears, extraction of the eyes. Insertion of the Little Piece of Wood into the Nine Entrances of the Body . . .

*Mod:*
All right den. I've got me mates here. (Pushes Ubu.)

*Ubu:*
Forward, Palotins, let the shittr-hook do noble battle!
(The Palotins rush forward waving lavatory brushes and start fighting with the Mods. One Mod falls to the ground. Others have got a Palotin on the ground and are putting the boot in. Père Ubu retires to the rear and shouts encouragement. One of the Mods sees him and rushes towards him.)

*Mod 2:*
I'll get the big feller.

*Ubu:*
No no don't hurt me I'm on your side Liverpool for the Cup I Love You Yeah Yeah Yeah Long Live King Billy. (By this time he is cowering behind Mère Ubu's skirts. Mod 2 pushes her aside and seizes him.)

*Mod 2:*
Yer dirty Prodestant bastard! (Butts him.)

*Ubu* (on ground):
Ooh, I'm dying. Our Phynancial nose, pride of our magnificent body, is irreparably broken. Help me, Mère Ubu!

CONTINUED OVERLEAF

*Père Ubu in Liverpool*

*Mère Ubu:*
Help yourself, you bloody great baby.
(The Mods run off. Palotins help Père Ubu to his feet.)

*SCENE THREE*
(Outside the Philharmonic Hall. Père Ubu, Mère Ubu and the surviving Palotins trudge along Hope Street. Enter a man in a bowler hat, morning suit, briefcase, rolled umbrella etc.)

*Ubu:*
Ah! At last a worthy-looking citizen. Obviously a Rentier, a man of substance in this city. Perhaps I shall now get some civilized directions . . . Excuse me, sire, but I and my entourage have walked for many hours and our Royal feet are exceedingly sore. Could you perhaps direct us to that which has heretofore been known as the Cathedral?

*Man:*
Yerwhar? (Ubu collapses.)

CURTAIN

*Adrian Henri*

**Sometimes**

Sometimes
I feel like a priest
in a fish & chip queue
quietly thinking
as the vinegar runs through
how nice it would be
to buy supper for two

*Roger McGough*

**Poem for Roger McGough**

A nun in a supermarket
Standing in the queue
Wondering what it's like
To buy groceries for two

*Adrian Henri*

## Still life poem

it might
be nature morte
but it's still
life

*Heather Holden*


## I Want to Paint

I

I want to paint
2000 dead birds crucified on a background of night
Thoughts that lie too deep for tears
Thoughts that lie too deep for queers
Thoughts that move at 186,000 miles/second
The Entry of Christ into Liverpool in 1967
The Installation of Roger McGough in the Chair of
                                    Poetry at Oxford
Francis Bacon making the President's Speech at the
                                    Royal Academy dinner

I want to paint
50 life-sized nudes of Marianne Faithfull
(all of them painted from life)
Welsh Maids by Welsh Waterfalls
Heather Holden as Our Lady of Haslingden
A painting as big as Piccadilly full of neonsigns buses
Christmas decorations and beautiful girls with darkblonde
                                    hair shading their faces

CONTINUED OVERLEAF

*I want to paint*

I want to paint
The assassination of the entire Royal Family
Enormous pictures of every pavingstone in Canning Street
The Beatles composing a new national anthem
Brian Patten writing poems with a flamethrower on disused
                                                    ferryboats

A new cathedral 50 miles high made entirely of pram wheels
An empty Woodbine packet covered in kisses
I want to paint
A picture made from the tears of dirty-faced children in
                                              Chatham Street


I want to paint
I LOVE YOU across the steps of St George's Hall
I want to paint
                pictures.


II

I want to paint
The Simultaneous and Historical Faces of Death
10,000 shockingpink hearts with your name on
The phantom negro postmen who bring me money in my dreams

The first plastic daffodil of spring pushing its way
through the OMO packets in the supermarket
The portrait of every sixth-form schoolgirl in the country
A full-scale map of the world with YOU at the centre
An enormous lily-of-the-valley with every flower on a separate canvas

Life-size jellybabies shaped like Hayley Mills
A black-and-red flag flying over Parliament
I want to paint
Every carcrash on all the motorways of England
Père Ubu drunk at 11 o'clock at night in Lime Street
A SYSTEMATIC DERANGEMENT OF ALL THE SENSES
in black running letters 50 miles high over Liverpool

I want to paint
Pictures that children can play hopscotch on
Pictures that can be used as evidence at murder trials
Pictures that can be used to advertise cornflakes
Pictures that can be used to frighten naughty children
Pictures worth their weight in money
Pictures that tramps can live in
Pictures that children would find in their stockings on
                                    Christmas morning
Pictures that teenage lovers can send each other
I want to paint
                pictures.

*Adrian Henri*


## Adrian Henri talking

I think it's part of a total life-style, really. You can't take my paintings without my poems. They are not meant to be supplementary in any way, but I'd like to feel that anything I wanted to do would come out in the most appropriate medium, that I could make a film about it, or write a poem, or do a play, or anything I had the technical capability to do. I'm interested in how a scientist would see it. A scientist would see literature of any kind, the printed word, or the spoken word even, as not being very different: all generically the same kind of thing, a form of communication. As a communication-mechanism, poetry in a sense is much more efficient than painting. Painting functions very differently. Poetry, particularly the way I do it at the moment, is not that often published and it *is* read out loud. It's like a telephone, you know, and a telephone is a perfect communications system. You put a message in one end and it goes through and comes out the other. Poetry is like that!

I think I get my values from painting. I read poetry as a sort of amateur. I've always liked reading poetry, but I was trained as a painter. The difference between painting and poetry to me is that painting's like a public address system —the message goes out but you're not aware of it being received, whereas in poetry you are aware of somebody at the other end of the telephone—at least in spoken poetry. Painting is very lonely: you do it in that room and then it goes away, goes into a gallery somewhere or into somebody's house, and you never see how they react to it really. You've got no way of telling what your paintings do to people, whereas if you read poems to an audience you can tell whether they hate them or not, or if they like them, or laugh at them. . . .

## Gloveparrot

I've been careless
I left my hat in the fire
The shape is there
but when I touch it
I am burned
The Japanese archer
stares at me from the
hill
I drive away
Hatless

*Spike Hawkins*

## Paste

The fish counted
up to 84 and then
fell off the edge
of the then known
        world

*Spike Hawkins*

## Richard

Irretrievable me
threw a stone in
a lake called
Sammy

*Spike Hawkins*

## Salad days 1914

The flags that were
furling fell from the
half mast and started
patting one another in
the bushes
quite softly to begin with

*Spike Hawkins*

## Tree army poem

Alert ruin!
They shout
from the trees
. . . stupid bloody acorns.

*Spike Hawkins*

## I sent a rich letter

Tasha I have won the goblet
and the free rosy plinth
Melissa sent a cable from
the Caribbean, it said 'Gratters'
The castle dance did swing

Were you tiddly, I mean stoned
Bunny Tucker is a stinker
Come and see my Goblet
I'm not washing since I
had the presentation
Man!

*Spike Hawkins*

## Clean

the sitting wreath
left by the well-wisher
drove off in a car
after him.

*Spike Hawkins*

## Bathchaps

The wooden scarves
they wear at college
do not creak in the cloister wind
but they do leave tracks
on the body
and when they come down
HEARTY
the tracks turn up
at the ends
Heraldic sorta thing
I suppose.

*Spike Hawkins*

LIVERPOOL YESTERDAY AND TOMORROW

## Adrian Henri talking

Do you know the funniest thing I know about an elephant was when I worked in this fairground in a seaside town years and years and years ago. This guy from Birmingham was there one year called Graham and he was incredibly short-sighted—he was the shortest-sighted person I've ever seen —and he broke his glasses somehow. He worked on the next stall to me and he went to get his glasses mended, you see. On his way back, walking along the promenade, he walked into an elephant. I mean, how short-sighted can you get . . . ?

## Summer Poems Without Words

(To be distributed in leaflet form to the audience: each poem should be tried within the next seven days.)

1  Try to imagine your next hangover.

2  Travel on the Woodside ferry with your eyes closed. Travel back with them open.

3  Look for a black cat. Stroke it. This will be either lucky or unlucky.

4  Find a plastic flower. Hold it up to the light.

5  Next time you see someone mowing a lawn smell the smell of freshly-cut grass.

6  Watch *Coronation Street*. Listen to the 'B' side of the latest Dusty Springfield record.

7  Sit in a city square in the sunlight. Remember the first time you made love.

8  Look at every poster you pass next time you're on a bus.

9  Open the *News of the World* at page 3. Read between the lines.

10  The next time you clean your teeth *think* about what you're doing.


*Adrian Henri*

Overleaf: THE BEATLES

## Roots

Roots were growing
            from my
        first pair of jeans
                but
I didn't tell
because I was afraid

        they'd laugh
        but now
since they've
        parking meters
        for life
they laugh
        because they are afraid
of running out of
        sixpences.


*Mike Evans*


## Song for a Beautiful Girl Petrol-Pump Attendant on the Motorway

I wanted your soft verges
But you gave me the hard shoulder.


*Adrian Henri*


## Morning Poem *for Dierdre*

'I've just about reached
breakingpoint,'
he snapped.


*Adrian Henri*


## My Johnny

My Johnny joined the army
Deserted me without a care
He got shot to ribbons
Now I wear him in my hair


*Roger McGough*

# Peeves

*Man:* Have you any pet peeves?
*Woman:* Yes, I have a pet peeve. His name is Spot and he lives on a strict diet.
*M.* What of?
*W.* Stricts.
*M.* And what else does he live on?
*W.* All fours.
*M.* But how does he sleep?
*W.* Soundly.
*M.* Is he house-trained?
*W.* He occasionally peeves all over the carpet.
*M.* Do you smack him?
*W.* On the spot.

*Roger McGough*

## The invention

Look at what I have just invented.

It is very interesting, what will you
call it?

I shall call it a wheel, it is for
getting about on.

It is a good name. But would it not be
better if you had four of them and then
put a motor car between, like other people?

What other people do is their affair, this is
my invention and I have not decided what to
do yet.

It is a very good idea, I am sure you will
make a lot of money from it.

We inventors do not make things for money,
but to improve living conditions for people
like you, who sneer.

I am not sneering, but it seems I have two
things rather like that on something I
invented, I call it a bicycle.

You don't care who you hurt do you?


*Henry Graham*

# She

1  How's your loved one?

2  My wife?

1  Your trouble and strife.

2  My run-for-your-life.

1  How is she?

2  Who?

1  Your wife.

2  Not very well as a matter of fact.

1  Really?

2  Well, you remember how forgetful she is.

1  How could I forget?

2  Well, I came home from work the other day and there was a note on the table.

1  A pound note?

2  Note at all. A written note. It said: 'Your dinner has gone to the hairdressers, I am in the oven'.

1  What did you do?

2  I went to the hairdressers for my dinner.

1  What did you have?

2  I had a short back and side of beef with shampoopadoms and bouffant potatoes.

1  Lovely. And how was your wife?

2  Done to a turn.

1  Did you have her for surgery?

2  No, I had her for supper.

*Roger McGough*

## Day off

1 Today, being sunny, I think I'll go down to the beach, take off my jacket, waistcoat and the top half of my undergarments and acquire a lovely tan.

2 Get all brown at your age?

1 What do you mean? It's easier at my age.

2 Demented, it's scrawled all over you.

1 What's that mean?

2 Like wrinkles.

1 No, don't like shellfish of any kind.

2 Today I'm going to take advantage of the special offers open only to children and old age pensioners.

1 Like what?

2 Like having my daily haircut.

1 You have your hair cut every day?

2 It's such a bargain, I can never resist it.

1 I think you're demented too.

2 Then I shall go to a matinee performance at a local cinema.

1 It's too sunny.

2 No, not when you're inside.

1 Tenpin bowling sounds nice—I'd like to try that some day.

2 It'd kill you.

1 Not if you're full of skill like I am.

2 'Ave you seen the balls they use? Heavy as lead they are.

1 That's right.

2 With little holes in which you'd get your arthritic fingers stuck.

1 Use soap.

2 So that when you bowled you couldn't let go and you'd shoot down the lane and disappear like a piece of soap down a plughole.

1 Plughole.

2 Then you'd be missing for weeks and eventually washed up on the beach at New Brighton.

1 Beach at New Brighton—how the 'ell do I get there?

2 Train's quickest, although if you were to go by bus you could take advantage of the special rates.

1 I might well do that.

2 Do what?

1 Go to the pictures.

2 Lovely day for it.

1 Lovely.


*Roger McGough*

## Adrian Henri talking

It's not that simple: on the one hand you can't not take the audience into account, and on the other hand you don't write purely and simply to impress the audience, or you'd write all funny poems—think of the funniest things you can think of, like vaudeville jokes I suppose, string them together and call it poetry. Or write all sad things. No, it's a bit more complex than that. I think that the whole modern tradition is writing for your own voice.

## Brian Patten talking

Yes, I read a lot in public—more or less make a living by reading. Read a great deal, you know. We did the Albert Hall; there was about 3,500 people. Then we do The Cavern, do universities and clubs, cover a large audience. There's a good response more or less.

## Adrian Henri talking

We have a sort of following, people who are mostly teenagers or early twenties, mostly non-intellectuals, the sort of intelligent beat music fans—the ones who choose between the groups, and don't just go for the one with a record in the Top Twenty—this kind of people.

## Roger McGough talking

At the readings we did every Monday night at Samson and Barlow's the kids didn't look on it as Poetry with a capital 'P,' they looked on it as modern entertainment, part of the pop movement. They may go away crying, or they may go away very sad, but it was a certain experience to them, all part of experience.